Tommy's Turtle

HOLT, RINEHART AND WINSTON, INC.
New York Toronto London Sydney

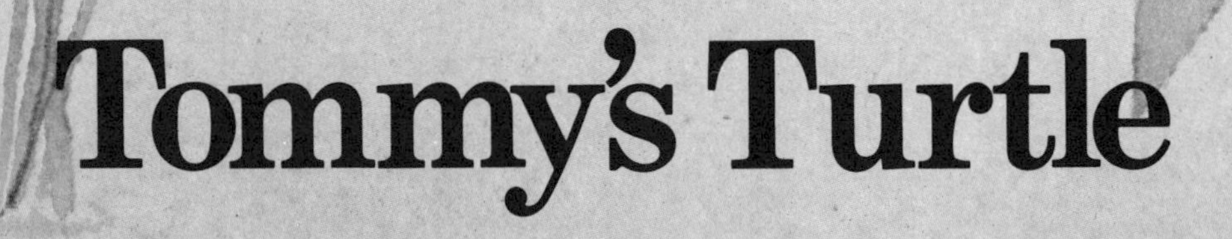

Tommy's Turtle

by Lawrence F. Lowery

Consultant, ABRAHAM S. FISCHLER

Illustrated by ELEANOR MILL

Printed in the United States of America

Library of Congress Catalog Card Number: 70-90441
SBN: 03-081182-1

90123 52 987654321

Tommy has a turtle.

One day when Tommy was walking home from school, he saw a brown and yellow rock. It was in a sunny spot near the pond.

Then something strange happened. The rock began to move.

It wasn't a rock at all. It was a turtle!

Tommy looked at the turtle. The turtle looked up toward Tommy.

It wasn't the biggest turtle Tommy had ever seen. It wasn't the smallest either. It was just the right size.

Tommy looked at the turtle even more closely.

Tommy noticed that the turtle had two hard shells. One shell covered the turtle's back. The other shell covered the turtle's underside. Each shell was made of smaller parts.

Tommy's turtle had four legs with claws on the end of each foot. Tommy also noticed that the turtle had a tail and a beak with no teeth.

Tommy put the turtle in a glass tank. Then he put water in the tank and a few large rocks. He tried to make the glass tank look like the side of a pond.

Then Tommy invited his friends to come to see his turtle.

Now that Tommy has a turtle he likes to watch it.

Sometimes the turtle swims around the rocks. At other times it climbs up on the largest rock and goes to sleep. When the turtle wakes up, it splashes back into the water.

This makes the water move. "How strange!" thinks Tommy. "The water moves and it isn't alive. The turtle moves, too."

Does moving make a turtle alive?

Once in a while Tommy takes his turtle out of the tank. He is careful to handle the turtle gently. Then the turtle crawls along the ground. It crawls the way it swims, by slowly moving its legs.

Do you think Tommy's turtle is alive?

One day Tommy puts his turtle upside down. The turtle moves its legs and stretches its neck way out. It tries to turn over. Then Tommy helps it.

Only a turtle that is alive can move its legs and neck.

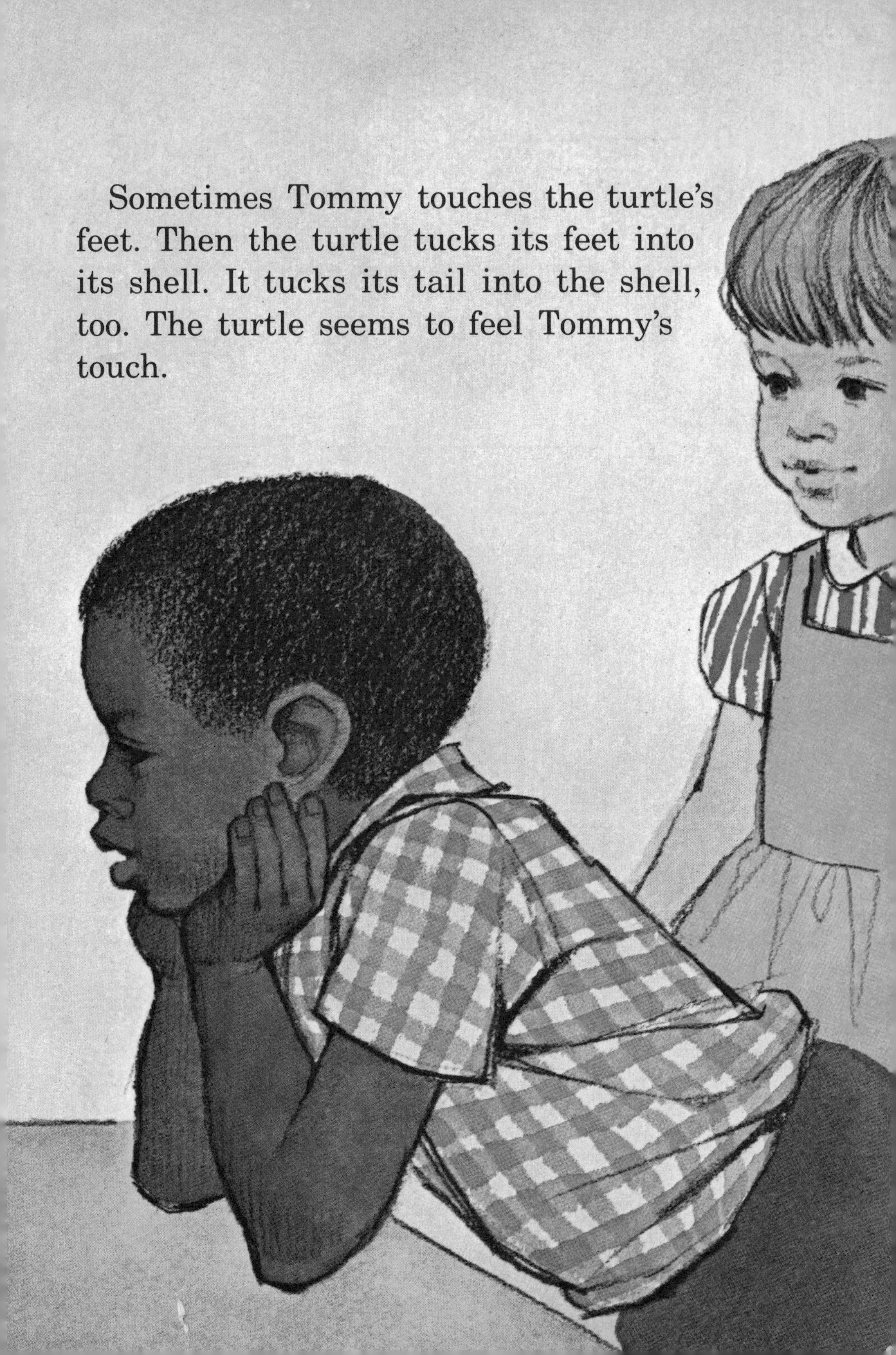

Sometimes Tommy touches the turtle's feet. Then the turtle tucks its feet into its shell. It tucks its tail into the shell, too. The turtle seems to feel Tommy's touch.

In the water and on the ground, Tommy's turtle can twist its head. It can stretch its neck far out and look around. Tommy can see it watching. He can see it blink its tiny eyes.

Tommy's turtle can do many things. "I like having a live turtle," Tommy says to himself.

Tommy feeds his turtle chopped meat tied on a piece of string. The turtle takes only tiny pieces. It uses its beak and its claws to break up the meat. It can bite and it can eat.

A turtle has to eat. "I wonder if this is what makes a turtle alive?" thinks Tommy.

Once Tommy's turtle was even smaller than it is now. Tommy's turtle has grown. Tommy grows, too. Food helps a living thing grow.

Food is something a living thing needs.

Sometimes Tommy's turtle swims underwater. It hides among the plants on the bottom of the tank. You can tell it's there when tiny bubbles of air come from its beak. Tommy's turtle can breathe air.

Tommy spends many happy hours with his turtle.

Sometimes Tommy puts his turtle in a pile of sand near the pond. He watches his turtle dig and crawl. He sees a trail the turtle leaves in the sand.

One day Tommy finds some tiny eggs in the sand. He asks his father about them. Another turtle laid them in the sand. Inside each egg is the beginning of a turtle. When the eggs hatch, out will come little turtles.

Tommy knows his turtle is alive.
It swims and crawls.
It eats and sleeps.
It sees and breathes
and grows bigger, too.

Tommy named his turtle Timmy.